The beginning and the end

September 12, 2021, it all ended…it changed…it broke us. 11:28 pm …. Or as my Marine would have said, 23:28.

My son's story is a beautiful one. He was a dedicated and decorated Marine. He loved his country and his family & friends. He LOVED Bentley, his black lab. Pieces of his story will be scattered throughout this, but this is primarily for you moms (and dads and sisters and brothers) who need to be reminded that you can still have joy while suffering immense pain.

Funny stories, words of wisdom, rantings and scripture will fill these pages and hopefully make you laugh & cry and remember you're not alone.

On the darkest day, please know that I am praying for you and all who grieve.

January 2022 – The "Safe" word

After leaving Arlington National Cemetery following our son's burial, my lovely sister -in- law suggested that we consider having a "Safe" word. A word we could say to each other to let the other(s) know we're having a bad day….a tough time…..because it's not easy to say "hey, help me. I'm at the bottom and I don't know what to do". But with the safe word, that person knows that you just need someone to sit with you in silence.

Thus, the origin of "Pineapple". God loves my in laws and outlaws. They have always been there for me. And in my darkest time, when I could not care for my husband and grown daughter, they provided what was needed. Handed me water and made me drink it. Made the food, banners, memorial gifts for our son's celebration of life….traveled across the country to be by our side on a moments notice.

And they are about the most inappropriate group of humans known to mankind. But they're my humans.

Actually Pineapple is not our safe word for our grief…..that we keep close to our hearts. However, Pineapple is the safe word used for another sister - in- law. She has no filter, has a heart of gold, snorts, and has a voice like a megaphone. "Pineapple" doesn't stop her, but it warns the others that something, likely X-rated, is coming.

Life lessons – Volume One

1. Family is everything
2. Some friends ARE family
3. It is very satisfying to meet up at a red light with the car that passed you
4. I notice that wisdom and grey hair comes with an interesting assortment of moans and groans
5. I'd marry my husband again in a New York minute
6. My children are my greatest joy
7. Some people suck but that's their karma
8. There is always room in my heart
9. Service to others is serving God
10. My outlaws keep me sane and embrace the crazy

11. My dogs believe that I am the coolest person alive
12. You will always have the best hair day on the day you think about canceling your appointment (don't)
13. Flossing is important
14. No one can see your worth but they can feel it
15. Energy and life only change forms; they never end
16. Kicking the snow clumps from your car wheels feels good
17. We are all someone's greatest love and someone else's nemesis
18. Nothing makes you wake up faster than a puking dog
19. Nothing puts you to sleep like a running fan
20. Dark chocolate is the best....white chocolate isn't chocolate
21. There are Angels among us

Journaling

Ick. I didn't want to do that. It wasn't going to help me, but they gave me this really cool book so I thought I'd give it a try.

Wow.....it's powerful. I can scream in my writing...I can swear the bad words I can't say in Panera....I can write letters to my son and to those who hurt me.

For me, I found that journaling helped me document events. As every grieving parent knows, your short term memory is shot! Some days I'm like Rainman but most days I'm glad I wear sandals rather than shoes that tie.

I like writing letters to my son and God. Releasing the thoughts to paper frees up some space in mind for new memories. The old are not forgotten but I think (for me anyway), writing them down made me feel safe. Like I'd never lose those thoughts when so many other things enter and leave my mind and memory quite freely.

So, give journaling a shot. No one has read my journals…it's just for me. Now, don't tell my therapist that it was a good idea, ok?

The Stolen Future

That's a tough one. There's no way to recover it.

The hugs I'll no longer get; the text messages that no longer "beep" on my phone; the missed phone calls; the holidays that suck now. Christmas, Thanksgiving, birthdays, Mother's Day....they're all too painful.

But it's difficult for "them" to understand ("Them" are those people who are fortunate enough to not be in the grieving parent club). But that's ok, you do you anyway. If you want to skip Christmas or start a new tradition, do it.

For us, we spend our son's/brother's birthday and anniversary days together…doing things that he would enjoy.

This often involves a pedicure (he was all about self-care) and a hamburger. Likely one of few people who'd go to Buffalo Wild Wings craving a burger! We laugh and cry and tell stories and share memories. This is what our new future is.

We're still adjusting to it.

WWBD

What Would Blaine Do? That's the mantra for our nonprofit as we evaluate grant requests. There are other criteria of course, but the bottom line is WWBD.

After Blaine died (several months later) I tried to figure out how to navigate this road. I decided to be present in order to survive. For me, I volunteer a lot....and I retired. A message came to me that this is what I needed.

I do "hard" things.....things that Blaine might do, or at least would tell me not to be afraid of doing. The only way I can find to continue to be his parent is to honor him through service to others.

Life Lessons, volume 2

1. True beauty has nothing to do with your physical appearance.
2. Always wear sunscreen
3. Don't take yourself too seriously
4. What other people think about you is none of your business
5. A deep breath and a big sigh feels fantastic
6. Sometimes not being invited is a gift
7. Give more than you take
8. Go to the zoo
9. Flossing is still important; have annual health screenings
10. Buy the hat
11. Give without judgement
12. Dogs are some of the best people

13. Family is everything.....by birth, blood, adoption, marriage, or just showing up
14. Death is not the end even though it sometimes feels that way
15. Do hard things
16. Give yourself the same graces you give others
17. Just because it fits doesn't mean you should wear it
18. Have a favorite number
19. A cryptic facebook post can drive people crazy and that's part of the fun
20. Laugh more than you cry
21. Tomorrow is not a guarantee (IYKYK)

Don’t worry about it, Mom

Oh, how many times I’ve heard this! I can hear his voice saying it. Some days that’s all I need to hear.

Speaking of hearing, I hear his voice often (not often enough). But his words have helped me through some tough times. One in particular, I was asking both he and God to help me with a difficult person who was causing me pain. As loud and clear as my screams were after his car accident, I heard, just as clearly, his voice say “mom, I need you to carry this burden for me”. You can’t say no to your son.

This sucks!

Yep. It really does. Then one day your survival will be someone else's road map for their journey. And let's be clear, it's a journey THROUGH AND WITH grief, not a journey PAST grief.

Proverbs

I was drawn one evening to read some bible passages. So like every good Catholic girl, I googled the passage I was looking for.

"He who follows righteousness and love finds life, prosperity and honor" Proverbs 21:21

This was my son. I don't think you could find anyone who would say he was anything but honorable. God needed him Home. "Death before Dishonor", one of his many tattoos.

Life Lessons, volume 3

1. I need to know that you care before I care that you know
2. Sometimes the people you feel are most unlikely to be compatible with you can be your touch stones
3. A new box of crayons is exciting, no matter your age
4. A gift should be given, not asked for
5. Always let the person telling the joke give the punch line....don't spoil that
6. Be your own advocate
7. Advocate for someone who can't
8. Eat dessert
9. Have at least one person you can depend on to identify that pesky chin hair, and return the favor

10. Let a child read to you
11. Read to someone who can no longer read
12. Give without rules
13. Make homemade frosting
14. Laugh more than you cry
15. Volunteer….for anything you are passionate about
16. Be the person other can count on
17. Say “yes”
18. Put your face in the sunshine
19. Say “no”
20. Let them…..
21. WWBD

God has already written the story

No matter how much you negotiate with God, to spare your child, even offering yourself, the story is already written.

I believe that when my time here is over, God will bring me Home. I did think that God and I would have discussed my son's death in advance, but I have learned that my faith is stronger than I knew (for which I am grateful).

Faith over fear. Good over evil. Truth over lies.

Where do you go from here?

Boy, I wish I knew. I can only tell you to turn to the people who show up for you.

A good friend told me that once you lose a child your address book will change. That is the truth. Some pages have been completely removed yet my address book is bigger than ever before.

Someone much greater than me said, People are in your life for a reason, a season or a lifetime.

Recognize those “lifers”, while appreciating those that were there for only a reason or season.

Life lessons, volume 4

1. Peace is often unappreciated
2. No one goes broke by being charitable
3. Have a ride-or-die friend (or maybe 2 or 3)
4. Lie down next to your dog and you'll discover a great listener
5. Tell a loved one you're proud of them and why
6. Journal (don't fight it….do it…it's only for you)
7. Feel the pride in your own survival
8. Split dessert
9. Spread good news
10. Say thank you
11. Sometimes you can laugh at a tongue twister for days
12. Make hard choices
13. Teach a child to make and count back change
14. Sometimes a pizza IS a single serving

15. Appreciate a great set of bed sheets
16. Never lie
17. Write thank you notes
18. Don’t worry so much about being perfect and start celebrating all the things at which you are excellent
19. Volunteer
20. Some people are mean…they are not your people
21. Always remember…

I am broken and unashamed

What you see is what you get. I no longer have time for trivial things...for arguing, hating, gossiping, hurting. Life is too short.

If you loved who I was before September 2021 and hope that one day that person will return, don't hold your breath.

I am broken and unashamed. I am who I am.

I also apologize for every thank you that I didn't say, every call I didn't return, every letter that wasn't written. But I'm doing the best I can.

In return, I will return every grace that is given to me.

Suicide

You didn't see that coming did you? For each of you struggling with grief, depression & anxiety please seek help.

Call 988. Talk to your partner, friend, family, clergy. We want and need you in our lives.

Unfortunately, our family has lost loved ones to suicide. We miss you every day. We will honor you by helping others.

#LRH

#AJQ

Thank you.

Thank you for reading the rantings of this grieving mom. Maybe some of these so called seeds of wisdom will help you. All profits from the sale of this book will go to the Blaine Halvorson Memorial (bmhmemorial.org), a non profit providing support for Minnesota veterans in crisis and other veteran charities.

~~Mel

Acknowledgements & Credits

All credits and acknowledgements are given to God for his graces and blessing.

I also want to thank my family and friends....none of whom knew that I was writing this.

Thank you to:

*Jerry

*Mickaela

*To our brothers and sisters, in laws and outlaws (too many to name individually, but the group is mightier than the individual)

*BHM Board members

*Bert for telling me what to do when I didn't know what to do next.

!!!! Pineapple !!!!

IFYKYK = 21

WWBD

Made in the USA
Monee, IL
19 November 2023